HEART MATTERS

HEART MATTERS

Jonathan Greene

[signature: Jonathan Greene]

BROADSTONE BOOKS

Library of Congress Control Number: 2007943554

ISBN-10: 0-9802117-0-0
ISBN-13: 978-0-9802117-0-2

Broadstone Books
An Imprint of Broadstone Media LLC
418 Ann Street
Frankfort, Ky 40601-1929
BroadstoneBooks.com

FOR BOB ARNOLD

IN TANDEM COUNTRY COUSIN

———————————

'…and if the heart
joins in the conversation,
the choice of words
won't be hard.'

—Ayya Khena

CONTENTS

I

II

JAPAN SKETCHBOOK

CHINA SKETCHBOOK

III

ACKNOWLEDGMENTS

The author would like to thank the following publications and their editors for publishing many of the poems in this collection:

[Ted Kooser] *American Life in Poetry:* 'At the Grave' was the second selection of this on-line column that is also printed by newspapers nationwide and beyond.

[Keith Flynn] *Asheville Poetry Review:* 'Holding Hands During Last Days,' and 'The Art of Invisibility.'

{Sylvester Pollett] *Backwoods Broadsides Chaplet Series, Number 100, Songs of Travel* by Jonathan Greene: 'Another Voice,' '*In the temple garden,*' 'Talking to a Monarch,' 'Ecumenical Liquidation Sale,' 'Heart Matters,' 'Overheard,' '*Snow,*' 'Starting with Lines from Chang Heng's *Fu on the Eastern Capital,*' '*The giant Buddha,*' 'The Hope,' 'When the World Ends,' 'The Time We Live In,' and 'To Change the Way You See the World.'

[Margaret Rabb] *Blink:* '*Grasshoppers,*' '*Wading into the river,*' and 'From Floorboards to Rafters.'

[Scott Watson] *Bongos of the Lord, (Sendai, Japan):* '*The giant Buddha,*' '*In the temple garden,*' and 'Starting with Lines from Chang Heng's *Fu on the Eastern Capital.*'

[Larry Moore & Steve Taylor] Broadstone Books published my version of the poem by Han-Shan in my *Gists Orts Shards, A Commonplace Book.*

[Sally and Sam Green] *Brooding Heron Press:* 'Supplication of the Dysfunctional Husband,' was solicited for a portfolio of Valentine's Day poems given to Ted Kooser who has for many years written poems to celebrate that day. Brooding Heron published *Out of that Moment, Twenty-One Years of Valentines* by Ted Kooser in 2006.

[Chris Green] *Coal: A Poetry Anthology*, Blair Mountain Press reprinted 'To Those That Refuse.'

[Richard Owens] *Damn the Caesars:* 'Wild Mushrooms,' 'To Those That Refuse,' 'Dynasty 101,' 'Portrait with Sports Jacket,' 'The Time We Live In,' and 'High School Memoir.'

[Julie Johnstone] Essence Press *(Edinburgh, Scotland)* published 'Ice Storm Damage' as a foldout booklet titled *Ice Storm.*

[Becky Hagenston] *The Jabberwock Review:* 'After the Funeral.'

[Paul Holbrook] The King Library Press published 'Fuji-San' accompanied by a photograph by Dobree Adams as part of the portfolio *Gnomon Press XXXX.*

[Bob Arnold] Longhouse published the booklet *The Death of A Kentucky Coffee-Tree & Other Poems:* 'Color Conflagration,' 'The Death of a Kentucky Coffee-Tree,' 'Donkeys Wallowing,' 'By the Ocean,' and 'Kentucky River Palisades.' Longhouse also issued 'Pond' as a postcard in their *Love Thy Poet* series.

[Philip Rowland] *Noon (Tokyo, Japan):* '*Moon caught in sycamore branches.*'

[Bob Arnold] *Origin:* 'Inch Work Yoga,' 'Always There,' 'Nothing to Hide,' 'Alone in this World,' 'Injunctions,' 'The Beauty of Verdigris,' and 'Taste of Spring, Winter Back.'

[Sebastian Matthews & Ryan Walsh] *Rivendell:* 'Listening to Mahler's 10th,' 'Dance Routine,' and 'Poets as Thieves.'

[Jerry Redden] Tangram Press published 'Death Postures' in a fold-out of my *Three Poems from Little Buck Creek*. Tangram also published '*Untangling this*' and 'Anyway' as small cards and 'Parable of the Famous Poet' as a large broadside.

[Michael O'Connor] *Vigilance:* 'In Old Japan.'

'First Light,' 'Allen Pond,' 'Pond,' and 'The Fire Rivers of Padma' were all collaborations to go with weavings and photographs by my wife, Dobree Adams. Thanks to Dae Gak and Robert West for their help. And, as always, to Dobree as well.

I

HEART MATTERS

for Bob Arnold

Each word
a messenger

asking you to be
a companion

on this hike
towards heart

fullness.

VISITING THORNS & PERRY

Drive
1,000 miles to

wake to the
same birdsong.

DON'T BELIEVE YOUR EARS

At times
the wind in the leaves
sounds more like rain
than the rain in the trees
in the wind.

TASTE OF SPRING, WINTER BACK

When a Winter day
warms to Spring weather,
the birds come to sing their Spring songs.

Next week when snow flies again—
the songbirds vanish, the harsh winds
make the trees dance in place.

NOTHING TO HIDE

for the mountains blasted
out of existence by mountaintop removal

The fog is out of a job—

all those mountains
it no longer shrouds.

BEYOND THE CLEARING

The crickets take refuge
in the tall grass
the forest shadows.

Their song silences
when storm clouds
hide the moon.

ROUTES

Hummingbird treading air
in the geraniums, bees
in their bee-balm namesake
plying their trade routes,
Marco Polo—a turtle
journeying to our pond
from some great distance.

MEMORIAL DAY HIJINKS

Thankful for drone
of 17-year-locusts
drowning out armies
of four-wheelers
on the distant hill.

OVERHEARD

Gee's Bend, Alabama

Strange,
some of
those days—
when we had
more of nothing—
we happier then
than now.

Wading into the river,
the mating dragonflies
sit on my wrist.
A voyeurism I don't
know what to do with.

TALKING TO A MONARCH

Butterfly
on my knee,
how was Chiapas
this winter?

Did you catch a ride
on top of a laundry basket
on top of the head
of a pretty girl?

Next year
gently brush her
ear and cheek for me,
por favor.

ARCHAEOLOGY OF OUR LOVE

At summer's window
the luna moth,
otherworldly,
comes to us

as if accompanist
to our trembling
first touch—fingers
alight so slightly

each
        to the
                other
to where we live.

BEACH TABLEAU

The crashing waves
disguise
      two brothers
yelling, sea bird
cries
     no matter
which.

KINGDOMS OF SAND

Words infused with such weight
that for ants building their sand castles
each grain were as a granite boulder

and all books—castles in the sand
awaiting storm surge. And all poets should
be named Anonymous or Ozymandias.

BEACH WALKING

So much beauty evanesces
like foam lace
the incoming tide
is busy tatting.

But before you capture
one eyeful, it falls apart,
intermingles with what
the next wave brings.

An art with no staying power,
that makes no claims upon the world
and is not seen as art, wraps around
your ankles. One more thing

to make you love this world.

LIKE, BUT UNLIKE

Wintering in Florida,
summers in New England,

the wild geese, like the rich,
have two homes,

but without the ostentation.

PASS IT ON

Question a gull,
'When's high tide?'

'Gotta go—

Ask the waves.
They'll know!'

A JOB FOR THE AGES

The insatiable need
of the unrelenting surf
to turn all rock,
from the pebbles
under our toes
to the fortress-like jetties,
into sand.

THE BOATS

When the storm surge came,
the water whisked away some
of the fishing boats
and hung them high
in the trees. Other boats,
mired in sand and staying put
looked anomalies,
until coming closer we saw
their hulls were rotted out,
their ribbing fractured skeletons,
anchored without anchor,
nestled in their uselessness,
their adventures forgotten tales.

SO IT GOES

The bottle corked
with its urgent message
crashes upon its
foreordained rocky shore,

shatters, the message lost.
As if unrequited love
needed one more
hopeless example.

BY THE OCEAN

The wave that knocked you silly
now a small puddle
waiting for high tide
to catch a ride back
into immensity.

CHTHONIC CICADAS

Orphic calling cards.

Suddenly gone.

Rethinking silence.

COLOR CONFLAGRATION

Sun setting,
the iris by the pond
up for the competition.

ALONE IN THIS WORLD

Forlorn, alone,
udder weighed down with milk,
trying to nudge her stillborn lamb
into life.

Grasshoppers
in such numbers
the high summer grass
talks like the wind.

CRITICAL TIME

The fish becalmed,
eyes adjusting
to this new world
after its furious rebellion,
tail flailing to no avail.

Assaying its length,
the fisherman once again
uncomfortable,
must play god.

FROM FLOORBOARDS
TO RAFTERS

During the barn dance

the barn

dances

THE SMUDGE

A tiny insect,
almost invisible,
died when last
I closed this book,
the telltale sign
we've been here
before.

INCH WORM YOGA

— Ω — Ω

Its whole life
this strange walk

from straight line
to omega

repetitious as
breath.

THE CAUTIOUS

After a rain
the elders
carefully avoid puddles,
walking the hump
in the middle of the road.

While the children, laughing,
jump into pot holes,
mud splashing their clothes,
not understanding our strictures
against such obvious fun.

CHILD'S PLAY

A stone's throw.

The children are trying
to fill the pond with rocks.

The impossibility of the task
does not bother them.

Their attention wanders—
now throwing a bucket of water

at the cat, who wanders off.
What next?

HIGH SCHOOL MEMOIR

That one in the back row
daydreaming, scribbling away,
that must be me!

ALWAYS THERE

Think of antique nested babushkas

or the equivalent grandfather figures.

Inside   inside   inside   the last one—
ourselves, the child we never left behind

intact.

ALCHEMIST COOKBOOK
RECIPE FOR IMMORTALITY

The elusive ingredient:
a peck of dust from the wings
of an angel.

DISDAIN SET IN STONE

All the world going past,
hardly a soul notices
the gargoyle above,
its tongue stuck out,
grimacing.

UNKNOWINGLY

When young—
a blank slate,

the unlined face.
Middle-aged,

face & voice,
the very gesture

of a grandfather's
hands

slicing the air,
all as if in homage.

FRAMED

Growing old,
you miss your mother
more & more.

Looking in the mirror,
more & more you
see her there.

DEATH POSTURES

Some animals
splayed out
as if on an
operating table

but the smaller ones
mostly fetal
as if hugging themselves
for a safe passage.

AT THE GRAVE

As Death often
sidelines us

it is good
to contribute

even if so little
as to shovel

some earth
into earth.

ONE NEVER KNOWS

The mink
hungers for
the blood of hens—

not the hanger
in a dark
penthouse closet.

After the funeral
everyone's boozing,
yapping about this & that.

Only the old man's dog,
sulking off in a corner,
is still in mourning.

THE HUSH AT SUNSET

The birds have quit their songs,
the deer kneel down to sleep
in the camouflage of leaves,

the clouds are deciding
just how many stars
to unveil.

Moon caught in sycamore branches.
When the tree sways with the wind,
the moon breaks free.

She worries:
a light left on
in the truck's cab.

I tell her:
the full moon
is in the driver's seat.

ANYWAY

The snail
leaves a trail

despite:
no followers

admiring
its self-containment,

patience,
its opalescence

the moon's light
polishes.

The full moon—
owl's accomplice
in the hunt.

ICE STORM DAMAGE

Life at times
tenuous
(refusing bad news)—

blossoms
on the cherry tree branch
hanging by a tenuous thread.

Mice in the walls,
bats in the eaves.

We built a humble home
for ourselves,

                a mansion
for them.

A LITTLE NIGHTMUSIC

The bullfrog's basso
anchors the high trill
of a chorus of peepers
forecasting a thunderstorm
coming over the hill
to silence this light overture
with Wagnerian weather.

THE HOPE

Morning glories
in winter, past glory,
vestiges of vines.
No one mourning.

But in summer
the possible resurrection
of their blue intensity, skin
tender as an eyelid.

PAVING THE WAY

Geese flying south.

Cold winter
hitchhiking on
their tail wind.

Snow
bends the daffodils
like a humble
Bodhisattva
kissing earth.

Snow peaks
slice the clouds
seamlessly.

The morning sun erases
what some artist with
painstaking strokes—
on each blade of grass—
painted with frost.

Untangling this
fishing line

makes reading poetry
seem easy.

II

JAPAN SKETCHBOOK

IN OLD JAPAN

Grass hat
thatch hut
over head

FUJI-SAN

Mountain's
mountain.

DAYTIME ROBBER

The thief forgot
one thing—
moon in the window.

—Ryōkan

Reflected
in the eye
of a dragonfly—
distant mountains.

—Issa

The giant Buddha
at Kamakura
looks down on
all who come
to visit.

He neither approves
nor disapproves.

Nonetheless.

He is there for us.

In the temple garden
no one told the cat
Buddha's lap
is off-limits.

CHINA SKETCHBOOK

ON THE DAXI RIVER

On remote terraced hillside farms
two objects are ubiquitous:

the full-size color poster of
Chairman Mao
facing the front door,

the mildewed satellite dish
tossed on top of an
outbuilding's tiled roof.

The family pig sty
the only traditional
accessory.

FARMERS MEETING THE LOCAL FERRY

Coming down steep trails
to the Yangtze

back-breaking loads
bob above

the undergrowth.
Only later can you make out

the person bent over
beneath, bearing this load.

Here is a tree, older than the forest it now shades,
its years beyond count.

Its roots, gnarled by the twists and turns of its soil.
Its leaves have known wind and frost.

The world derides its scarred bark,
cares nothing for the fine heartwood within.

With all its bark stripped off, a patina shines.
What remains—a core of truth.

—*after Han Shan*

STARTING WITH LINES FROM CHANG HENG'S
FU ON THE EASTERN CAPITAL

With action not getting much done,
Everyone busy without much to show
    but death and destruction....
There is a deep longing for peace,
A nostalgia for the quiet times
    of the Dictator, whose cruelty
    we knew how to live with,
    beneath notice, not speaking our thoughts.
As before, we are always being watched
    by enemies, friends alike.
But the fear is death by a fluke of crossfire
    coming back from market
    with some simple necessities.

❖

DYNASTY 101

Everyone bows
to the Emperor,
he to no one.

A tradition
thousands perished
upholding.

IN THE MUSEUM OF MACAO

A display of cricket cages,
carrying gourds

to take prized crickets
to high-stakes cricket fights,

elaborate
cricket coffins,

the losers sleepless in
a silent house.

III

TO THE READER

All your doors locked,
barricades around the heart,
ears plugged as if a chorus of Sirens
are luring you to destruction
on their rocky perch,
your eyes tracking any route
that may need to be retraced
out of captivity—

my poem's simplicity
fashioned to find
a way in, beyond
your fear against
such openings.

But then you are
in a hurry to ignore me,
while I have the patience
of timelessness and wait calmly
till you tell me at last that
you need to listen
after all.

ART

Life came, asking:

Show me as I am!
Oh, I know you cannot
help idealizing, throwing
hyperbole my way.

I am your model, naked,
plain, waiting to be
transformed, transfixed,
falsified.

A mirror midwifing
another mirror.
Endless births.

—after Rafael Alberti

FIRST LIGHT

Tenuous first sun
before its strong beam
has climbed over
the hill.

Birds tune up
to full strength,
while the cock
tones down his rhetoric.

The mountains
await their green dress.
Soon the work of the world
begins again.

A BUDDHA MEETS A STOIC

Life—
a life & death struggle
which dictates an urgency
to stay calm

to see clearly
the landscape / inscape
we walk in outside / inside
attach / detach

inhale / exhale an equanimity
that gives the firing squad
of our enemies no victorious
exhilaration.

SAINTS

They had skeleton keys
to open the doors
of all hearts

and yet they were
kept waiting,
the unsure exiting

back doors,
sending alms
via the butler.

ECUMENICAL LIQUIDATION SALE

On one store window
a Buddhist truth emblazoned:

EVERYTHING MUST GO!!!

above another sign
with a fringe Christian message:

FINAL DAYS!!!

KENTUCKY RIVER PALISADES

Water is a sculptor
carving this limestone edifice,
working with haphazard weather,
meticulously searching for weakness
in rock. It will take ten generations
to note the next stroke of genius.

TO CHANGE THE WAY YOU SEE THE WORLD

Sanctify the smallest thing,
this smooth stone, for instance,
a tiny seed spit out by Ice Age gears
of massive rock, then polished
in mountain creeks for centuries,
waiting for you to pick it up
for a pocket charm, only to lose it
rolling down the hill giddy with first love
and that she took that leap first
and you followed laughing and crying
to the bottom where the road begins.

THE DEATH OF A KENTUCKY COFFEE-TREE

Fallen, the large tree
that owned this domain.
Its root ball—flesh-colored
arthritic spikes
that had dug in for its
goodly time.

Seeing daylight
synonyms death.

Saplings that had stunted
in its shadow sing hallelujahs,
compete for new light.

ALLEN POND

Cherokee National Forest, Tennessee

The pond
an eye
that reciprocates
the sky.

AT BURLEY'S POND

Turkey buzzards stationed
on fence posts,

wings spread as if
laundry drying.

As long as I walk
with stealth

and have no camera
they pose, photogenic

as all get out.
I click this poem.

POND

Mirror, clock of
sun and moon
in their diurnal dance.

Window, a look in
at the koi, visible only
when the water warms.

Habitat for turtle & frog,
who journey to land
quite differently:

one with a lumbering
tenacity, the other jumping
into Spring.

Pond, a multi-tasking passive
genius with no Mind of its own.
Life-giver, taking all the hillside
donates, charity begun in the heavens.

THE WATERFALL AT BAD BRANCH

Recalling a visit with Dobree and Dana

The drought
has tamed
the waterfall's thunder

to the trickle
of a faucet
seven-eighths
shut.

Its fierce redundant
rhetoric subdued,
its message can now
be deciphered:

I learn by repetition.
I have the power to wear away
the hardest obdurate rock.
One droplet the moss weeps

at first light can hold
an unseen rainbow
on its journey
back to the sea.

COLD FRONT

In an oasis of drought,
the congregation of leaves
sway with a prayer
for rain.

The flowers open their palms,
spokesmen for parched roots,
the needs of pilgrim bees
knitting an interwoven world.

All heads turn upward.
Only rain can save this brown world,
cleanse its air, cool its feverish brow
with a healing insistent patter.

CAMPING OUT FOR THE FIRST TIME

I make a tent in my bedroom
by tying two ends of a blanket
to the radiator and weighing down
the others with volumes
of the *Encyclopedia Britannica*.

I raise the blinds to let moonlight
fall through the thick forest. Pine scent
from a pine needle pillow near my head.
I bring my flashlight in to read by
and in case of bears.

Sleeping on the forest floor
is sort of rough, so I hike
back home and sleep in my own bed
the next night and all the nights
after.

THE HANDING DOWN

He raises his son
to breed pigeons
carrying messages
from a Brooklyn rooftop.

Years ago, his mistress
(recently arrived
from the old country)
took his messages to heart.

This, the only tryst
for their forbidden love:
reunions that were carried out
by these tiny beating hearts,

birds with an instinct bred back
in the ruins of Time.

DONKEYS WALLOWING

The donkeys bathe in dust,
the one spot in the pasture
that shines bright on
full-moon nights.

Moved to another pasture,
they will excavate another crater,
grunt with pleasure scooting
along the ground on their spines,

then rise with festive brays and stand
again, refreshed. Giving the donkeys
a good pat, generations of dust rise up,
coughing out a cloud that engulfs us.

Heirloom carpets that have
never been cleaned, they are soon
back to their non-stop grazing.

WILD MUSHROOMS

for Mark Hedden

Miracle out of earth and air,
with rain, shade, tree bark, duff,
filtered sun in token amounts,
all in just the right haphazard portions
so this moment happens.

Nothing tastes more of earth.

The moment gone. More leaves fall.
The mushrooms evanesce, as if they never were,
gone without trace, but for spores—
ghostseeds dreaming
next year's serendipity.

SAVORING THE SCRAPS

My grandfather carved
the crust from the bread.
My favorite. I ate it up.

My wife, making pie,
gives me the apple peel
she pares off in an endless S.

Give me your discards.
I will digest and
savor the scraps—

those secret untold stories
no one has time for,
all my favorite starting points....

REPAIRING BOARD FENCE

In mud, ice, & manure
we play 'Nurse, forceps please'
with hammer and crowbar.

Just one of the dances
of our love.

To sleep again without worry
as the horses browse
moonlit grass.

BY HEART

Another familiarity, knowing these old songs
by heart. Unrehearsed, not knowing
the other knew, songs of mothers and fathers,
songs whose tunes have been simmering
somewhere in the blood before the words
resurface.

Songs from some great distance, from some
years between wars we did not know
and even so, a shared memory. Seeds planted
by others, a preliterate childhood radio
Judy Garland visited, 'Over the Rainbow'
siphoned out of invisible air waves

to radio consoles. Radios that welcomed every morning,
where a Tower of Babel started rebuilding, ground floor
rising from rubble, brick layers / disc jockeys /
newsmen troweling the mortar of palaver,
the glue all the small talk barbers / hairdressers
would use for starters all week long.

Then in the evenings, so many of our songs,
often just little snippets, fragments of melody,
will bring us back to what matters:
what our hearts have learned by heart.

SUPPLICATION OF THE
DYSFUNCTIONAL HUSBAND

for Dobree on Valentine's Day, so she has a poem
from my hand, in addition to one from Ted Kooser

Complete my sentences.
Give my thought the word
I cannot grasp.
Remember the names
of my second cousins
once-removed and on what
obscure branches of the family tree
they perch....

And I will sing your praises
in some out-of-the-way publication
from a troll laboring at a handpress
on some faraway island.
                              [No less.]

GULFS

'attention exactly between the words' —ANSELM HOLLO

THE WOMBAT HIDES FARTHER
TO SLEEP IN THE SHADOWS

Awareness | a wariness

SHIKANTAZA

Inaction | *in action*

BYSTANDER | ACTIVIST

Apart | A part

FAUX HOMAGE

Walden Pond | Waldenbooks

DAYDREAMING DEVELOPER'S EUREKA

hickory glade | Hickory Estates

REAL ESTATE OFFICE SIGN, MARS HILL, NC

Homes!!! Land!!! | homeland

WILL DAY'S REFUSE TURN INTO NIGHT'S DREAM

Inedible | Indelible

ONE AT A TIME

in between deaths | be in breath

GENTLE SNOWSTORM

Each snowflake kissing your face
dies a unique death, each loss
lasts its sweet nanosecond,
the architecture of its beauty lost
unseen under microscopic camera,
your bloodheat speeding its extinction,
a sacrifice of an instant/infinitesimal/infinite
good-bye with a sweetness overlooked
as a picturesque winter scene from above
but below savored as a memory of
such a sweet pastoral time in
a heart's memory.

DANCE ROUTINE

The snakeskin
attached to a piece
of split cherry
thrown on the fire
rises up and does
one final eerie dance
up into flame.

He who sloughed this off
lies asleep up the hill
under a rock outcropping
waiting for spring
when I will start to build
his summer woodshed home
out of new firewood.

PORTRAIT WITH SPORTS JACKET

The sports jacket
is cattywampus on its hanger
as if it were walking down
a midnight street
with too much to drink
and lungs full of cigarette smoke,
with lost friends and family
no longer a possible angelic choir
singing Requiems or the Górecki Third.

But the body from inside the jacket
finds comfort in his bed
like a familiar love that accepts him
without conditions or complaints—

a life all cutting room floor material
from his own B movie.

RESTLESS CITY PAST MIDNIGHT

About the time the firemen quit their poker game, a night watchman enters an office building to man the front desk of Absence.

In the shadow of garbage cans a cat–rape–cry that's over before one can ascertain its painful truth.

The last drunk wakes to a bartender turning down the lights, locking up.

In cubby hole apartments how many restless sleepers suspicious they have taken the wrong path?

POETS AS THIEVES

OR A PRIMER FOR A WALK
WITH WORDSWORTH & COLERIDGE

I steal your best image,
making a better poem,
and you reading this
steal it back transmogrified,
a startling brainstorm, *why did I not
think of that before* (forgetting
that you had).

I find your poem better than I could
ever hope for...

until in dream a lightning bolt hits,
how to polish this further,
a new immortal line,
a radiance only I could envision....

Etc.

As if all together we are writing
just the one poem
looking for the Editor beyond us
to fuse the diamond.

PARABLE OF THE FAMOUS POET

When the famous poet is born in this province and moves to another at two weeks, both provinces will always claim him as a native.

When someone misquotes the famous poet, despite denials from the poet, this misquote will dog his days, survive him into posterity.

When the famous poet dies of a misstep on a cliff overlooking a creek in flood, many will claim he jumped, some will say he was pushed, others that he slipped. One version will be codified as the true one based on verification by someone who was not present.

The famous poet no longer recognized himself as he stood that day on the cliff, his followers having distorted all he had been saying all these years, quoting lines out of context to make a mishmash of whatever clarity he once strove for.

Then even his fame left him, diminished to a footnote in *One Thousand Ming Dynasty Poems* stating that he was thought to have influenced a poet well-represented in its pages but unknown in his lifetime.

THE ART OF INVISIBILITY

As a child, did I hide behind my parents not wanting to shake the hands of strangers? I was pushed forward.

In life I do not rise to the top as cream. Hidden in murky waters (my own, the river we live on) after a storm.

Nominated for top prize, I drop off the honorable mention list. After my name is spoken, it becomes a whisper, without echo.

Perhaps gesture is all? I could skywrite poems over vast desolate tundra or write in invisible ink, be the only one knowing what immortal words had vanished.

Those I once knew well have a habit of faintly remembering my name, nothing else. Or, not even that.

I will pass unnoticed, no burden to the chroniclers in later times.

Forget you ever read this.

THE BEAUTY OF VERDIGRIS

The tortoise moves slowly,
outlives us.

We look down on it.

The sequoia pierces the sky,
outlives us.

We look up to it.

In Japan, they revere ancient trees,
old folks. Rich patina of age.

Not knowing this, know less?

Youth passes us on double yellow lines,

dual exhaust blasting any comment
we might have.

A SHORT HISTORY OF ADULT LIFE

A lifetime surrounding oneself
with what one loves.

> *Diverting*
> *the stream.*

A crash course,
letting it all go.

> *Final potlatch*
> *into the hands*
> *of others,*
> *over the cliff.*

HOLDING HANDS DURING LAST DAYS
for Anne Frye

From under quilts and blankets
on a warm summer day
the long bony cold hand
reaches out to me.

Startled by the sensuality of its touch
in this leave-taking, never knowing if
it is to be the last. When these hands
say good-bye it is in stages

with stops on a downhill path
waiting to catch breath, and at each
the hands intermingling their own
unique erotic codes which in another

time and place could be read as flirtation.
But not now, her body wasted by cancer.
Yet a beauty in the midst. Envision in the guise
of an Andersonville/Auschwitz wraith—

an angel nimbus mixed with the horror of her
wasting away, body haloed/hollowed,
Rilke's *For Beauty is but the beginning
of terror*....

The double edged sword we lick honey from
and such sweetness cuts, awakens and shadows us.

THE SQUABBLE CONTINUES

She planned all the details
of her funeral. One was to buy store-
bought frames and have pictures of her life
on a table at the visitation.

She was estranged from her sister;
they fought for years over the spoils
left by their parents. Then
at the visitation, her daughter

spied her aunt cramming
the framed photographs in her handbag.
Just as her mother had warned, what
we had assumed must be exaggeration.

From beyond, perhaps there was whispering:
I told you to watch her, I told you so.

ON HER DEATHBED
in memory of C.R.H.

With the incipient signs of life supports—
oxygen, feeding tubes, monitors—
she wakes to our worried faces
and holds our hands to comfort us
as if to say it cannot be helped,
with imploring humor
mocks a helpless shrug—
while she still has this strength.

KEEPING TABS

How many newspapers
ricochet against the front door,
the paperboy daydreaming
baseball glory throwing
the runner out at home—

before a neighbor would notice
the scattered pile, realize
the old man had been
gathered up, would get
a few lines with a black border.

DIASPORA

Ensconced in my reading chair
at home. Even home—exiled.
A gypsy chord from Django,
an apt Yiddish word takes me

back into my birthright world
of ashes and survivor guilt.
Under the palimpsest of this day's
sidewalk and street

I am digging through rubble,
searching for the lost family,
as if I could ever hear the last echo of
childhood laughter the tanks buried.

A water witch looking for
ancestral rivers of blood.

EXECUTION IN THE MIDDLE AGES

The half-light inside the executioner's mask,
a hothouse of stale breath, the sweat-stained leather
against a two-day growth of beard.

As the rope is set, his last meal regurgitates.
Its rancid acid burns his throat. He thinks his innocence
a kinship to his Lord Jesus.

The blindfold, a prelude to darkness.
Hopelessness, a final refuge.
Drum roll quiets the crowd, erases thought, time.

SHOPPING FOR SHOES

(WAR BETWEEN THE STATES)

Having survived another battle,
shopping for shoes
among the dead.

Hurrying, before the stench rose,
remembering to breathe through
your mouth. Less stench in winter,
but the shoes harder to wrestle off.
Then often disgusted, to find their shoes
in worse shape than yours.

At times, the inevitable mistake:
a low moan, last small breaths,
eyes looking up into yours.

ANOTHER VOICE

To praise peace
in peaceful times—
a lantern lit at noon
on a sunny day.

To praise peace in war time—
a searchlight at midnight,
the dogs howl, the police
take you in for questioning.

TO THOSE THAT REFUSE

The cellist of Sarajevo, Vedran Smailović,
refused, insisted music transcend
the indiscriminate shelling
of the Innocents.

And in Tiananmen Square
the anonymous pedestrian
dared the tank
run over him.

Or in Knott County
the widow Combs
likewise dared
the stripmine dozer.

Or Rosa Parks
refusing to move
to the back of the bus
that Montgomery, Alabama day.

All saying no to the everyday
aggression of the Men of the Lie,
the business-as-usual
wrong-headedness of our worst ways.

In History these exemplars
to awaken the passive sleepwalkers
who live in days of terror, an acquiescence
to the nightmares of righteous wars

with the rationalism of knee-jerk patriotism,
no matter which nation rallies before which flag.

THIS WAR

In the White House high-fives
and yells to 'bring on the bubbly'
bragging what smart bombs
can do, war by remote control.

   The mothers are weeping over
   their dead sons, daughters....

The brothers of the slain
swear revenge, curse the infidels,
their own lives as naught, swear to avenge
this unholy aggression.

   The mothers are weeping over
   their dead sons, daughters....

Over oceans, enemies ignorant
of each other, rumors given credence,
hate the easy emotion, black & white
the only colors fundamentalists see.

   The inconsolable mothers' keening does not disturb
   the sleep of the self-righteous powerful.

LISTENING TO MAHLER'S 10TH

CONTRA RAINER MARIA RILKE

Yearning that yearns for more, that
even as consumed, wants to be consumed again.
The flame sputtering red to blue
to blinding torch-white purity
focused on the obdurate tissue
of his own heart.

Almost as if reaching the mountain top
he puzzled going beyond that height
with the Fool's almost suicidal balance.
So it is with absolutes and mortals
tempting the thin air of the gods,
Love given weight it cannot bear.

Borne, it leads to Rilke's trail of broken hearts,
the lonely trial of art in its tower seeking
a cold marble perfection with its bloodless
veins masquerading as life's rationale,
a poor human ration, a path without heart,
while under foot a gravity-fed spring pulses.

CHRISTMAS ICE STORM

A terrible beauty is born...
Sunday preachers with their
End of Days sermons,
a war of beheadings, a tidal wave
of death beyond imagination....

In such a time an ice storm,
God encasing each tree branch,
down to the smallest twig, in a translucent glass—
when the sun shines: blinding crystal,
under a full moon: another brilliance,
like an x-ray negative held up to a light box
in the darkened room.

The trees suffering under this beauty,
they bend, they bow, they break at
their elbows and wrists and ankles,
die a bloodless death (except the box elders
with their red hearts), die on board fences,
on the road, in the woods and pastures.

In the middle of the night trees halve
with the noise of cannon-shot,
making us wonder if the preachers
are right in their adumbration of Apocalypse,
though their pretty pictured Heaven *For Believers Only*
must only prove no one knows the future.

Mystery rules. Mystery trumps all.

INJUNCTIONS

Carve words into stone/paper
out of still wordless air.

Out of incessant chatter/war noise
link with a peace beyond.

Seek beyond the commonplace knee-jerk
with strange responses no one expects.

Realize the many ways: energy of hummingbirds,
dogged sloth of turtles, your own tropisms.

Be grateful each day for each day.
Praise all who populate its moments.

Forget injunctions.
A new hidden path in the underbrush!

WHEN THE WORLD ENDS

Digital clocks
go blank, rectangles
of nothingness.

The hands of old clocks
give us, in inexact
approximations,

the mute time of
History's final second,
and perhaps some

with an uncalled-for
extra effort push
one second beyond

out of habit, or
the usual reflex
of Denial.

THE FIRE RIVERS OF PADMA

Lifetimes,
the many mountains
traveled.

The valleys
of firestreams
crossed.

Though there are
forebears and friends, loves
as close as twins,

you are alone
on all your
final journeys.

THE TIME WE LIVE IN

Yggdrasill,
Great Tree of the World.

That world came apart, splintered.

Some pieces the tide brought in
used for kindling one long dark senseless night.

NOTES

OVERHEARD [p. 11]: I first saw the quilts from Gee's Bend, Alabama, in Milwaukee when I was there for the Lorine Niedecker Centenary in October, 2003. But it was when I ran into the show again at the Corcoran in Washington, D.C. in 2004 that I heard the phrase 'when we had more of nothing' in a video that accompanied the show. The quilts were 'saved' by Bill Arnett whom I met when Jonathan Williams took me to an open house Arnett was giving at his manse in Atlanta. He was vilified by *60 Minutes* on CBS for making money off of the Afro-American artists he represented. Later on *CBS Sunday Morning* he was lauded for saving the quilts from Gee's Bend. Still later the quilts were featured on postage stamps.

KINGDOMS OF SAND [p. 16]: Ozymandias is the name given to the Egyptian Pharaoh, Ramesses the Great, in the famous poem written by Percy Bysshe Shelley in 1817.

PASS IT ON [p. 19]: Adapted from a version of a Japanese folk poem in Eric Sackheim's *The Silent Firefly: Japanese Songs of Love and Other Things.*

ART [p. 72] was inspired by a poem by the Spanish poet Rafael Alberti (1902-1999), 'A la pintura' or 'To Painting,' but uses the original only as necessary armature to make a very different poem.

SUPPLICATION OF THE DYSFUNCTIONAL HUSBAND [p. 92]: The press referred to in this poem is Brooding Heron Press run by Sally and Sam Green on Waldron Island, one of the most remote of the San Juan Islands in Washington. See Acknowledgments for details of the occasion for this poem.

GULFS [p. 93]: *Shikantaza* is 'just sitting' or 'non-intentional sitting' Buddhist meditation. A term Krishnamurti used was 'choice-less awareness.'

TO THOSE THAT REFUSE [p. 112]. All the names in this poem were unknown until their spontaneous acts of heroism caught the notice of the news media:

On May 27, 1992 during the war in what was called 'the former Yugoslavia' twenty-two were killed by a grenade while waiting on a breadline in Sarajevo. For twenty-two days after this, at 4 o'clock in the afternoon, despite the risk to his own life, the cellist Vedran Smailović went to the massacre site and played his cello in memory of the dead.

On June 5, 1989, a man with a shopping bag in each hand, stood in front of a column of tanks the day after the Chinese ended their brutal suppression of the pro-Democracy demonstration in Tiananmen Square. The tanks were heading away from the Square down the 'Avenue of Eternal Peace' when the pedestrian suddenly stepped forward in a pedestrian zone. The head tank tried to go around him, but the pedestrian quickly moved in front of the tank again and again in no matter which direction the tank turned. The head tank stopped and finally turned off its motor. The pedestrian climbed up the tank and spoke to its driver and then returned to the street. Some came and led him away, either bystanders going to his aid so he would not be crushed by the tank or secret police taking him away to some unknown end.

In November of 1965, Ollie 'Widow' Combs was arrested as

she stood defiantly in front of bulldozers who were working for stripminers about to mine her land. She was protesting the possibility that boulders and debris from the mountainside would destroy her home as they had many others. At age 61, she was carried off her mountain and taken to jail. Bill Strode, whose photographs of this were to win a Pulitzer Prize, was also taken to jail for not giving up his camera. In 1977 a law regulating stripmining was finally enacted, though this victory has proven to be very limited.

Rosa Parks worked as a seamstress for a department store. and was on her way home on December 1, 1955, when she did not go to the back of the bus as the Jim Crow laws of that time and place dictated. She was arrested and fined. A few days later the Montgomery bus boycott began and an estimated 40,000 stopped taking the bus, some walking more than 20 miles to work. Finally on November 13, 1956, the Supreme Court outlawed segregation on buses. The order arrived in Montgomery on December 20th and the boycott which had lasted 381 days, ended the next day. Racist violence did not end as snipers shot into buses and bombs were tossed into Black churches and the homes of Black ministers.

THE FIRE RIVERS OF PADMA [p. 120]: 'Padma' (lotus) here refers to Amitayus (Tibetan: *Ce-dpag-med*), Buddha of Boundless Life, closely associated with the Dhyani Buddha Amitabha.

As heads of the Padma Buddha family, they are spiritual sources from which emanate the compassionate Buddhisattva Avalokiteshvara and Tara. Amitayus resides in Sukhavati, the Western Paradise, where those who invoke the blessings of Amitabha can be reborn. Rebirth in Sukhavati, where conditions are perfect for attaining enlightenment, is earned through merit and faith.

This poem was written to accompany a weaving by Dobree Adams.

THE TIME WE LIVE IN [p. 121]: Yggdrasil is the World Tree, a sacred mountain ash or rowan, that in Norse mythology was located at the center of the universe and spanned Heaven and Hell.